KATHERINE ROY
NEIGHBORHOOD SHARKS

HUNTING *with the* GREAT WHITES *of* CALIFORNIA'S FARALLON ISLANDS

DAVID MACAULAY STUDIO · ROARING BROOK PRESS

NEW YORK

EVERY SEPTEMBER the great white sharks return to San Francisco. Their hunting grounds, the Farallon Islands, are just 30 miles from the city.

While their 800,000 human neighbors dine on steak, salad, and sandwiches, the white sharks hunt for their favorite meal.

From sunup to sundown sharks
circle the shores, stalking their
unsuspecting prey.

They cut through the water in
total silence . . .

. . . until, all at once, they strike.

BUT HOW DO THEY DO IT?

It starts with the perfect meal . . .

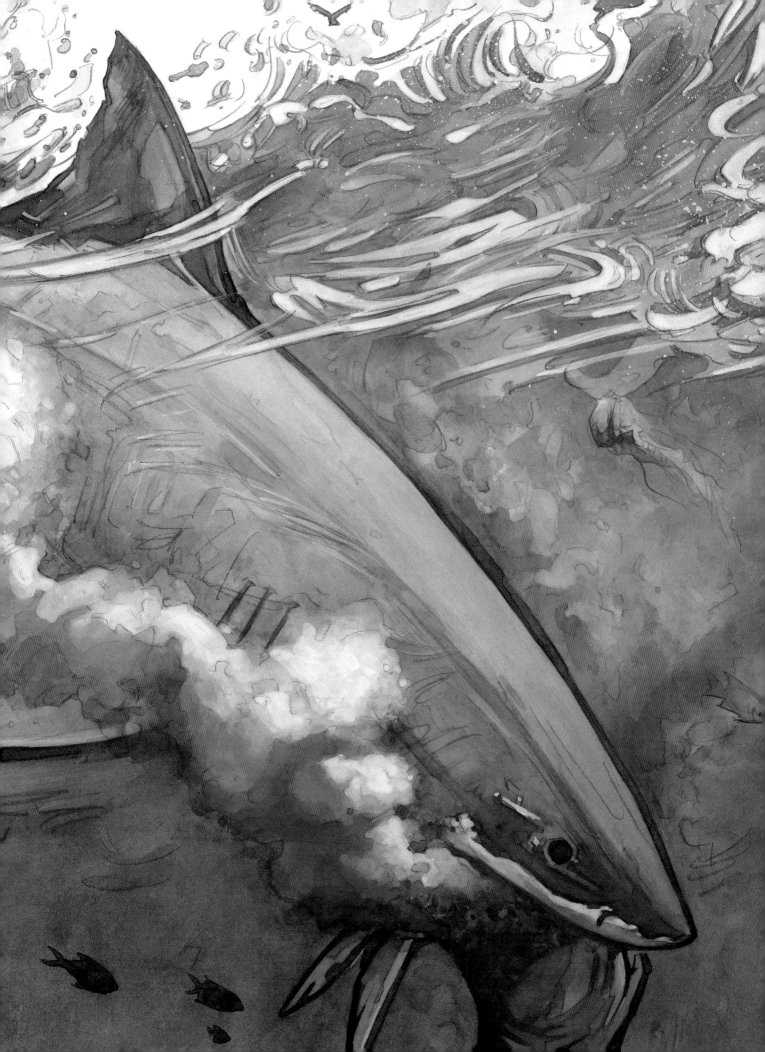

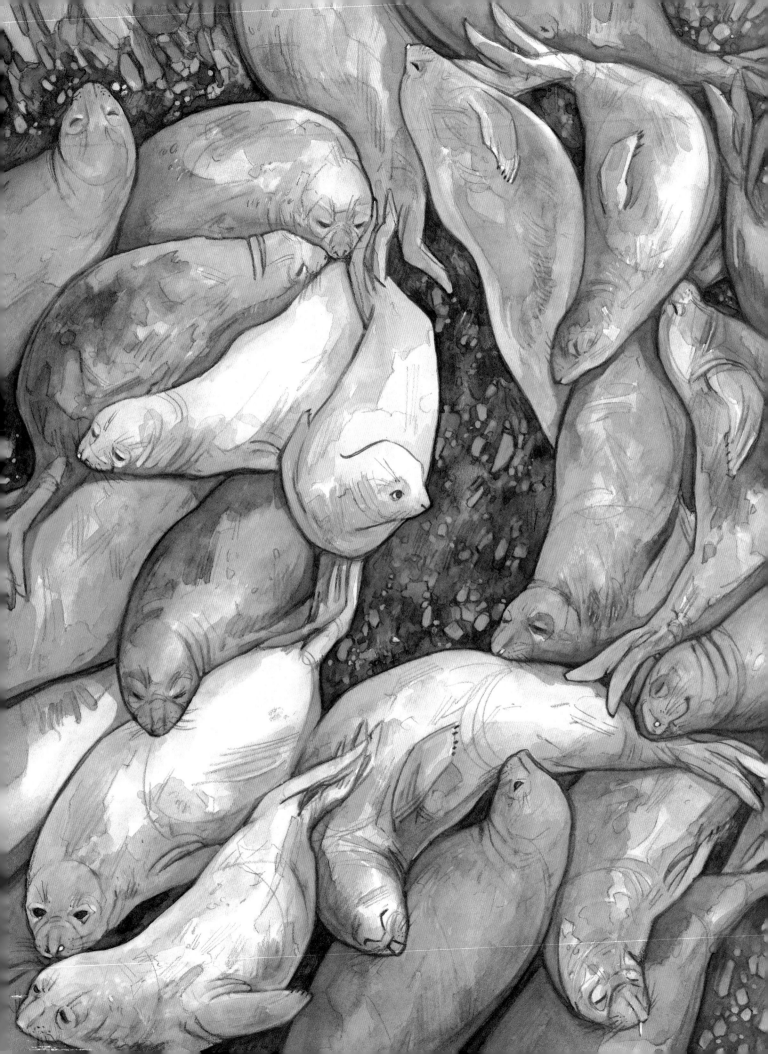

HOT LUNCH

EVERY YEAR THE FARALLON ISLANDS provide sanctuary for thousands of pinnipeds—a name for seals and sea lions that means "fin-footed." Northern elephant seals—so named for the trunk-like snout on the adult males—come to the protected Farallon beaches to breed and give birth each fall. Young elephant seals start arriving in September and must haul out of the water for the very first time. They weigh up to 400 pounds, have a body mass of nearly 50 percent blubber, and they often swim slowly and alone—in short, they're nature's perfect energy bar for a hungry white shark.

With a thriving pinniped colony, close proximity to San Francisco, and a seasonal concentration of some of the largest known white sharks in the world, the Farallones are one of the ocean's best hotspots for scientists to study white sharks in their natural environment. The sharks follow the seals, and the scientists follow the sharks, recording their feeding and behavior each fall. The smell of the seal colony initially attracts the huge, hungry whites, and then the hunt begins with a shark's first weapon of attack . . .

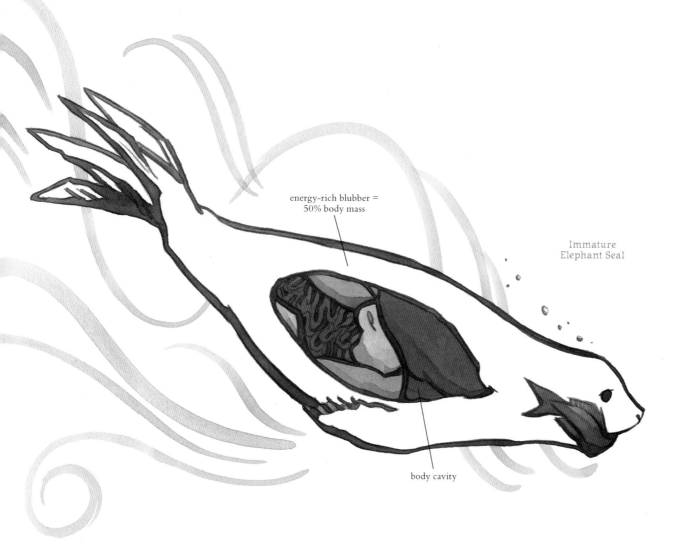

energy-rich blubber = 50% body mass

Immature Elephant Seal

body cavity

THE PERFECT BODY

WHITE SHARKS ARE THE LARGEST living predatory fish in the ocean, growing up to 21 feet long, 8 feet wide, and sometimes weighing over 4,500 pounds. Their torpedo-shaped bodies are adapted for highly efficient swimming, perfect for both endless cruising and bursts of attack speed out in the Farallones' Mirounga Bay. With just two flicks of its tail a white shark can reach speeds of up to 25 miles an hour, fast enough to leap out of the water or to ambush an elephant seal from below. The dorsal fin and keels give its body stability, while the paired pectoral fins provide lift in the water, like wings on a jet plane.

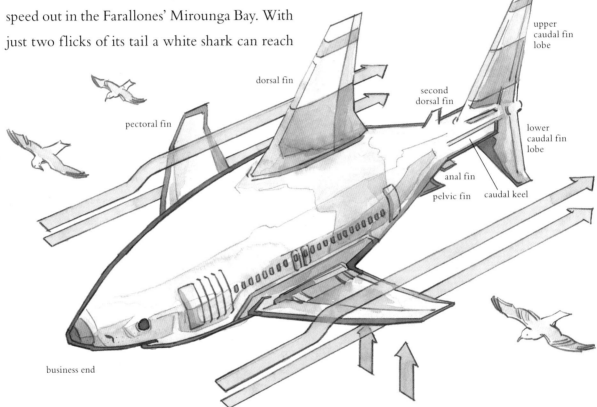

dorsal fin

pectoral fin

upper caudal fin lobe

second dorsal fin

lower caudal fin lobe

anal fin

pelvic fin caudal keel

business end

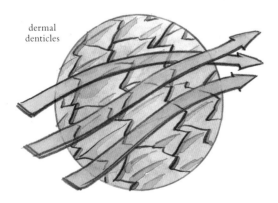

dermal denticles

White sharks are also covered in tiny scales called dermal denticles. Not only do these backward pointing "skin teeth" literally cut through water, they also serve as camouflage—a white shark's dark back and ghostly belly disappear against the Farallon reefs. But body shape can only go so far when it comes to catching mammals in the cold Pacific Ocean. To stay quick enough to keep up with their prey, white sharks have a second hunting weapon . . .

HOT HEAD

MOST SHARKS AND BONY FISH have blood that runs as cold as the ocean. With no blubber for insulation and chilly water flowing past its blood vessel–packed gills, a fish's blood travels from gills to body and back again at the same temperature as the surrounding water.

But a white shark's main blood vessel, called the dorsal aorta, is unusually small, forcing most blood leaving the gills into a tight web of arteries and veins that weaves through the shark's red muscle tissue. This web acts as a heat exchange system: the movement of the shark's muscles warms its blood, so the ever-swimming shark increases its body temperature just by moving!

With a resulting body temperature about 20 degrees Fahrenheit above the surrounding water, a white shark functions as a warm-blooded fish. The extra heat speeds up digestion and makes its reflexes lightning-fast, enabling it to catch and eat its warm-blooded pinniped prey. A warmer brain and warmer eyes also give the shark its third weapon . . .

dorsal aorta

gills

heart

cold water in

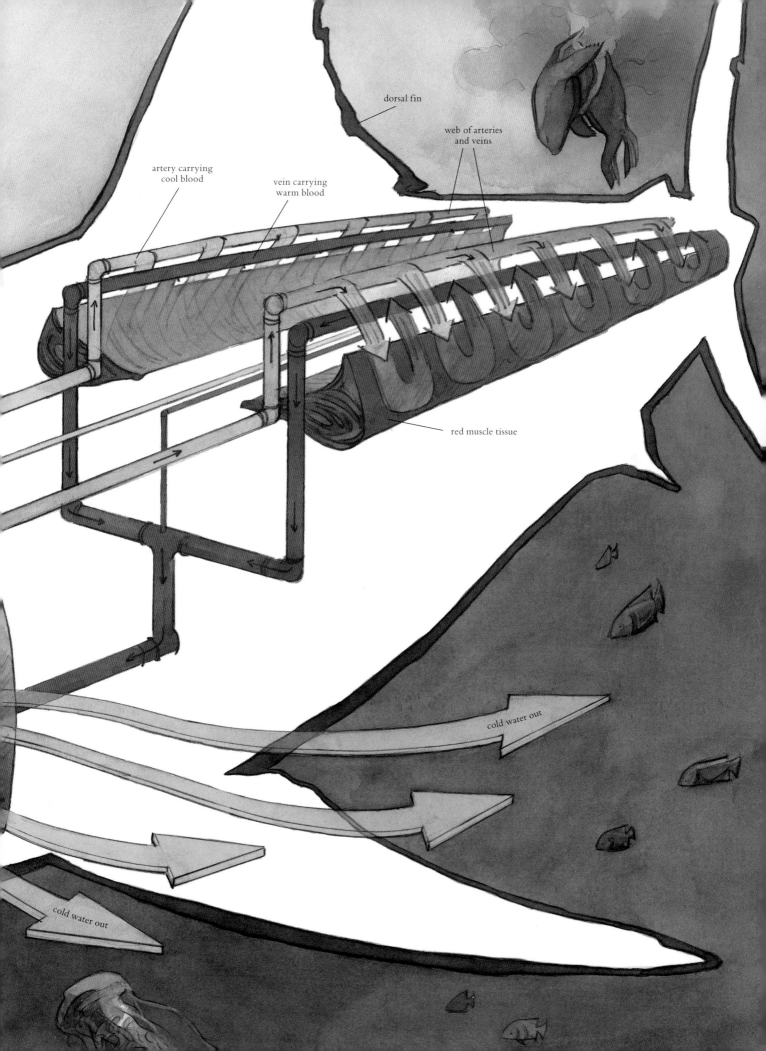

dorsal fin

web of arteries
and veins

artery carrying
cool blood

vein carrying
warm blood

red muscle tissue

cold water out

cold water out

cold water out

HIGH-DEFINITION VISION

WHITE SHARKS are visual predators—they target their elephant seal prey primarily by sight. Their small but highly sensitive eyes are equipped with two types of photoreceptors, called rods and cones, suggesting that their daytime vision is in high-definition with a limited range of color. This helps a white shark to better distinguish seal-like shapes floating at the surface. Adult white sharks may only feed every few weeks, so it's critical that they spend their energy hunting high-calorie seals!

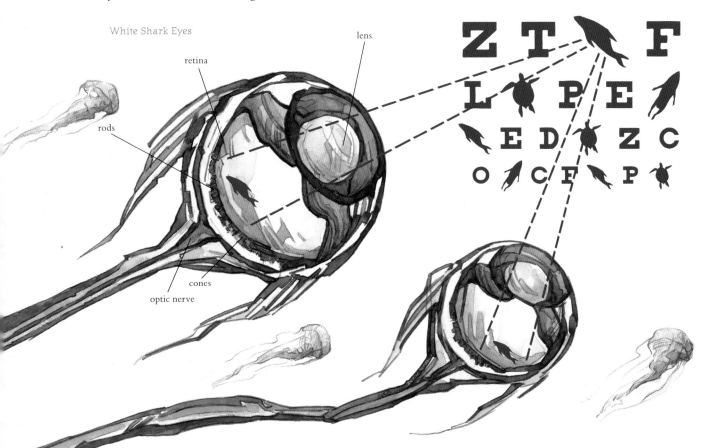

White Shark Eyes

retina · lens · rods · cones · optic nerve

A white shark's pointed snout enables binocular forward vision, so it can always judge distance when approaching a potential meal. In the instant before impact a white shark rolls back its eyes to protect them from being scratched by the claws and teeth of a thrashing seal—a one-eyed shark would not survive long at the Farallones. Electro-sensitive pores along the shark's snout, known as the ampullae of Lorenzini, take over for the temporarily blinded shark, locating the seal's living electrical field as they make final contact. Now the shark is close enough to kill the seal using its fourth and most intimidating weapon . . .

ENDLESS TEETH

CARCHARODON CARCHARIAS—the white shark's scientific name—comes from the Greek words for "jagged" and "tooth." Twenty-six top teeth and twenty-four bottom teeth flash from the front row of a shark's mouth and are designed to eat a variety of prey, from fish and rays for young sharks, to marine mammals for the adults, whose wider teeth tilt inward for bigger bites. By the time a white shark reaches ten years of age its teeth are large enough for a Farallon seal feast.

When a tooth wears down or falls out—which happens at nearly every meal—a new tooth begins rotating forward to take its place. This ensures that a white shark is always ready to dine with a razor-sharp smile. The shark seizes the unlucky elephant seal between its teeth and then releases the dying animal—which floats at the surface—and circles back to eat the seal with its final weapon . . .

five rows
of teeth

cartilage jaw

blood vessels

gum line

PROJECTILE JAWS

WHEN IT COMES TO EATING an entire pinniped, leverage is just as important as a face full of teeth. A white shark's jaws aren't fused to its skull, but can be projected forward to generate a maximum bite force. From first hit to last morsel, every white shark bite has a five-part progression that all occurs in less than a second. An adult shark can eat a 400-pound seal in under ten bites, with up to 50 pounds in each bite:

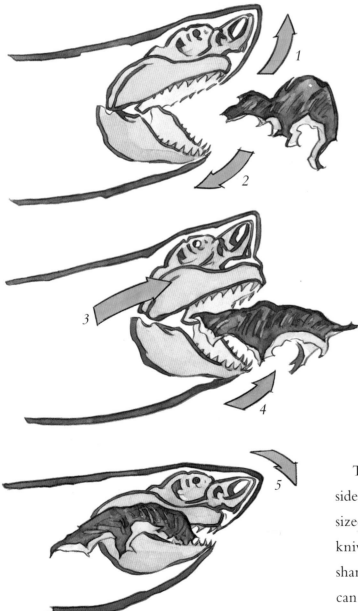

The white shark lifts its snout (1) to open wide—up to 40 degrees above its body—while (2) dropping its lower jaw.

The shark then thrusts its upper jaw out from its skull (3) while lifting its lower jaw (4), pinning its prey in place like a fork pinning food to a plate.

Finally, the white shark drops its snout (5), leveraging the force needed to cut through the elephant seal's flesh, bone, and blubber.

The shark then shakes its head from side to side while powering forward to shear off gulp-sized bites, using its upper teeth like a set of steak knives. It swallows its food whole—a white shark cannot chew at all. At long last the shark can enjoy the delicious seal . . .

BUT NOT SO FAST!

EVEN WITH THE PERFECT BODY, warm blood, sensitive vision, sharp teeth, and killer jaws, a Farallon white shark still has obstacles to consider, mainly competition from other white sharks for the right to feed. Attracted by the smell of blood in the water, neighborhood sharks quickly arrive for a bite of the freshly killed seal. Among Farallon white sharks, carcasses often go to the females, who grow two to three feet longer and weigh several hundred pounds more than the adult males. But rarely is there a direct fight between two hungry white sharks over food. Instead, the losing shark must swim on in search of a new elephant seal . . .

Back out in Mirounga Bay, the hungry shark
patrols the reef, hunting for another meal.
Armed and ready, it closes in on a new target
straight ahead . . .

TAG! YOU'RE IT!

REMEMBER THE SCIENTISTS who follow the sharks? They use a seal-shaped decoy made of carpet to lure the sharks to the surface. While the shark is busy tasting the dummy, scientists reel in the line to coax it closer to their boat, where underwater video and photographs are taken to later study behavior and distinctive body markings. The edge of a shark's dorsal fin is completely unique—as distinctive as a human fingerprint—so these photos are used to help identify individual sharks. Sometimes scientists attach a tag to the shark's dorsal fin using a long rod equipped with a small, dart-like tip. The dart both secures the tag in place and takes a tissue sample with a single prick.

Some of these tags are ultrasonic transmitters that send data to receivers anchored at underwater checkpoints. Others pop up to the surface and transmit signals to satellites after riding a shark for a set number of months. These tiny computers can take any number of readings, from the shark's exact geographic location to its speed, depth, and body temperature, and the temperature of the ocean. After nearly three decades of research, the Farallones' role in the life of a white shark is beginning to emerge . . .

float

accoustic tag

underwater receiver

anchor chain

FARALLON SOUP

EVERY WHITE SHARK is an "apex predator," meaning an animal at the very top of the food chain. But their supply of elephant seals all depends upon cold, nutrient-rich water that rides currents up from the ocean floor at the Farallon Islands. When this cooler water comes into contact with sunlight at the ocean surface every spring, tiny plants and animals called plankton burst into activity, making the ocean here like a rich, abundant soup! The plankton are eaten by fish and krill, which in turn are eaten by whales, sea birds, and pinnipeds. The sharks come for the seals in the fall, fattening up at their favorite seafood joint after spending many months offshore.

Maintop
Island

Mirounga
Bay

warm surface
water

Saddle Rock

wind

As predators, both the sharks and pinnipeds help keep the ecosystem fit—by eating their fill of weaker prey they leave healthy animals to breed new generations of young. Scientists estimate that only a few hundred individual sharks make up the entire adult and subadult population of white sharks migrating to central California. With so few sharks, each individual animal has a disproportionate impact on the balance of the Farallon food chain.

Lighthouse Hill

Southeast Farallon Island

cold water from upwelling

nutrients

phytoplankton & zooplankton

THE WHITE SHARK CAFE

BUT A WHITE SHARK'S part in the ocean's ecosystem isn't all patrolling for Farallon pinnipeds. White sharks are migratory animals—just like whales and many birds—and the electronic tags now make it possible for scientists to chart their offshore habitat. Though these sharks are capable of swimming anywhere in the ocean, dorsal fin photos and tags reveal that the *same* white sharks follow the *same* migration routes every year:

December–March: The male sharks leave the Farallones one at a time and swim toward a spot in the Pacific nicknamed the White Shark Cafe. Meanwhile, the majority of the females head for Hawaii, which may be a foraging area for moms-to-be.

April–July: At the cafe, male sharks spend their hard-earned seal calories rapidly diving over and over again while some females briefly enter and exit the area. Since the sharks eat half as much while offshore as they do at the Farallones, the cafe is most likely a destination for mating, not hunting.

August–November: The now-skinny male white sharks abruptly leave the cafe and individually migrate back to San Francisco to feed. Female sharks give birth every other year off the coast of Mexico after an estimated 12- to 18-month pregnancy, joining the Farallon feast on alternating falls when pregnant.

White sharks have circled the oceans for 11 million years—10.8 million years longer than people have walked the earth. But their small numbers, expansive range, and slow reproductive cycle make the species intensely vulnerable to our impact on the planet. Can they survive another 200,000 years of humans?

The ocean is a system, and understanding it and keeping it healthy is vital for both the sharks and for us. So this September—just 30 miles from San Francisco—the scientists will be waiting for the white sharks to return . . .

. . . and hunt for their favorite meal again.

SHARK UP! A NOTE FROM THE AUTHOR

On a clear day in San Francisco you can see the Farallones from the Golden Gate Bridge. The islands crouch like granite teeth along the rim of the continental shelf, and when you're out there on the water—still within the city limits—you feel as if you're floating at the edge of the world. What better place for the wildest population of white sharks on earth?

I grew up an hour south of San Francisco, but knew nothing about the islands before starting this project. A carefully protected National Wildlife Refuge, they are strictly off-limits to the public; the only people allowed ashore on the islands are the marine scientists lucky enough to stay for a season, who go for weeks without access to mainland food, water, or power. Farallon researchers are some of the most patient and dedicated field scientists there are. I never actually set foot on the islands themselves—there was no direct need for my book—but I had the extraordinary privilege of spending four days on the water in October 2012 with the Farallon shark team. I heard nearly two-dozen tagged sharks pinging the acoustic receiver, saw a shark named Tip Fin thrash a decoy, and witnessed several seal attacks from afar, complete with bright red blood and flocking seabirds. I watched the calculated drop of a new acoustic receiver, which was immediately followed by a line fouling our boat's propeller, and the complicated problem of fixing it without getting in the water with the sharks. I handled collections of white shark jaws, teeth, and fins, compared electronic tags, and later dissected a baby hound shark to get an inside look. A great many hours were spent observing the scientists' methods, and they were absolutely gracious in sharing their research with me—both published and unpublished—and in answering my endless questions during the three-hour trips to and from the islands.

It might be surprising to learn that Farallon scientists name the sharks that they study, but the animals live for so long and the population is so small that individuals quickly become familiar. Tom Johnson, a male white shark, was already full grown when he was first sighted in 1987, and every year that he returns he sets another longevity record. How long do white sharks live? How often do they eat? How and where do white sharks mate? The only way to get an in-depth understanding of the way they live is to study the same sharks year after year. So far, no human has ever seen a white shark mate or give birth.

The Northeastern Pacific population of white sharks currently has more protection than any shark species frequenting California's coast. While there may be no immediate threat to the Farallon adults—it is unknown if their small numbers are normal or critically low—southern Californian and northern Mexican coastal waters are a shared nursery for newborn sharks. White sharks aren't mature until they reach eight to twelve years old, and without healthy new recruits the Farallon shark population will not survive, so overfishing regulations in both the U.S. and Mexico need steady monitoring and reinforcement. Oceanic scientific study has barely begun, and our understanding of this precious resource is central to the long-term survival of the Farallon whites. We humans are guests in the water, but the sharks call it home.

A FEW WORDS ON SMELL

After much consideration I decided not to include a full spread on a white shark's sense of smell. Sharks use different senses at different distances, and though scent is an invaluable tool there is little data on exactly how they use their olfactory system, and you can't train a white shark or keep one in captivity for long enough to find out.

A substantial percentage of their brain is dedicated to smell, and it may prove to be used just as much for long-range navigation, pheromone detection, and reproduction as it is for tracking prey. But the final moments of the hunt are visual, and I wanted to tell the story of one shark hunting one seal.

SELECTED SOURCES

I consulted dozens of books, scientific journals, websites, apps, documentaries, and raw footage as I wrote and drew this book. Some of the most helpful were the following. For a complete list of these sources, please visit my website, katherineroy.com.

Anderson, S., T. K. Chapple, S. J. Jorgensen, A. P. Klimley, and B. A. Block. "Long-term Individual Identification and Site Fidelity of White Sharks, Carcharodon Carcharias, off California Using Dorsal Fins." Marine Biology 158 (June 2011): 1233–1237

Jorgensen, S. J., N. S. Arnoldi, E. E. Estess, T. K. Chapple, M. Rückert, S. D. Anderson, and B. A. Block. "Eating or Meeting? Cluster Analysis Reveals Intricacies of White Shark (Carcharodon carcharias) Migration and Offshore Behavior." PLoS ONE 7(10) (October 2012): e4781

Jorgensen, S. J., C. A. Reeb, T. K. Chapple, S. Anderson, C. Perle, S. R. Van Sommeran, C. Fritz-Cope, A. C. Brown, A. P. Klimley, and B. A. Block. "Philopatry and Migration of Pacific White Sharks." Proceedings of the Royal Society B 277 (November 2009): 679–688.

FURTHER READING

Over the last three years of working on this book I've fallen head over heels in love with learning about white sharks (and sharks in general). To learn more about them, I highly recommend the following resources:

FILMS

The Great White Highway: Where the White Sharks Go. Discovery, DVD, 2012.

The Great White Shark: Truth Behind the Legend. Paul Atkins, National Geographic, DVD, 1995.

BOOKS

Ellis, R., and J. McCosker, Great White Shark. Stanford University Press, 1991.

Jorgensen, S. Sharks: Ancient Predators in a Modern Sea. Firefly Books, 2013.

Klimley, A. P. and S. Oerding, The Biology of Sharks and Rays. University of Chicago Press, 2013.

ONLINE RESOURCES

Shark Net app (for iPod and iPad)

California Academy of Sciences (Check out their live Farallones webcam): calacademy.org/webcams/farallones/

The Farallon Islands: California's Galapagos, web video: science.kqed.org/quest/video/the-farallon-islands-californias-galapagos

Farallones Marine Sanctuary Association: farallones.org

TOPP (Tagging of Pacific Pelagics): topp.org

Monterey Bay Aquarium: montereybayaquarium.org

Point Blue Conservation Science: pointblue.org

ACKNOWLEDGMENTS

These pages would not have been possible without those who so generously gave of their time and support, and I am endlessly thankful to the following people: David Macaulay, my mentor for over a decade, who with his imprint has heartily welcomed me through yet another door; Simon Boughton, my ever-listening editor, who gifted me with an offer for this book on my birthday; Stephen Barr, my amazing agent, whose guidance at every step helped turn a pile of sketches and notes into a real project; Andrew Arnold, book designer extraordinaire, and the rest of the terrific folks at Macmillan.

To Ron Elliott, my liaison to the sharks, for his insight, courage, and friendship, whose stunning cageless footage of Farallon whites let me see below the surface; Scot Anderson, pioneer Farallon shark researcher and rock star naturalist, for inviting me aboard to first see the islands and for openly sharing his expertise (along with his fabulous collection of jaws and bitten surfboards); Sal Jorgensen, Taylor Chapple, and Paul Kanive, for looking out for my safety, sharing photo resources, and for so patiently explaining how tagging works and what the recent data means; John McCosker and the California Academy of Sciences, for the tour of shark specimen archives and for the hands-on dissection of a baby hound shark; Russ Bradley, for his steady enthusiasm and for connecting me to the Farallon team; A. Peter Klimley, for his research help; the crew of the Derek M. Baylis, for your hardwork and safe passage to and from Mirounga Bay; to TOPP, Hopkins Marine Station, the Monterey Bay Aquarium, Point Blue Conservation Science, and the Farallon Island National Wildlife Refuge; and to Sicklefin and the other sharks who showed up on the last day—your curiosity and grace while swimming under and around our tiny boat still takes my breath away.

To my incredible friends who lent direct help to this project: Maris Wicks, Paolo Rivera, Karen Shaw, Jon Chad, and Laura Terry; to the Elliotts, the Roys, and the Stouts, for providing the ultimate Bay Area home base. And lastly, to my wonderful husband, Tim Stout—dedicating a book full of blood and teeth to my spouse might seem strange, but for his companionship, collaboration, critical eye, and enduring support, who understands my love of wild and beautiful things, this book is for him.

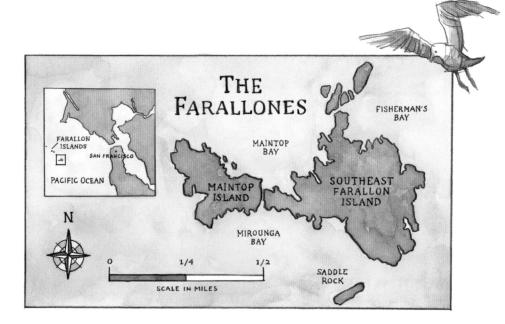